STEAM
AHEAD

EXPERIMENT WITH

KITCHEN

SCIENCE

Inspiring | Educating | Creating | Entertaining

Brimming with creative inspiration, how-to projects, and useful information to enrich your everyday life, quarto.com is a favorite destination for those pursuing their interests and passions.

Author: Nick Arnold
Illustrator: Giulia Zoavo
Cover design: Sarah Andrews
Design and Editorial: Starry Dog Books
Consultant: Pete Robinson

© 2019 Quarto Publishing Group USA Inc.

This edition published in 2022 by QEB Publishing,
an imprint of The Quarto Group.
100 Cummings Center,
Suite 265D Beverly,
MA 01915, USA.
T (978) 282-9590 F (978) 283-2742
www.quarto.com

A CIP record for this book is available from the Library of Congress.

ISBN 978-0-7112-7981-0

Manufactured in Guangdong, China TT012022

9 8 7 6 5 4 3 2 1

MIX
Paper from
responsible sources
FSC® C016973

Picture credits
All photographs by Starry Dog Books
with the exception of the following:

SHUTTERSTOCK
Cover Akom Somsamai; 17 b/g D. Pimborough; 18 Esmeralda Edenberg; 20 b/g EldoradoSuperVector; 24 Oxy_gen; 28 b/g thidaphon taoha; 32 b/g CK Foto; 34 b/g Anusorn Nakdee; 40 b/g Olga Hmelevskaya; 44 b/g white snow; 46 b/g mim.girl; 57 zkruger, 64 Ryzhkov Photography; 66 b/g Didecs; 70 5 second Studio; 70 b/g Stone36; 70 Valentyn Volkov; 76 Svetlana Foote; 76 Moving Moment; 76 Olga Popova; 79 Ryzhkov Photography.

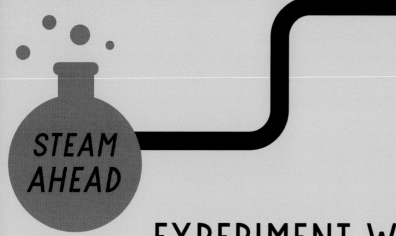

STEAM AHEAD

EXPERIMENT WITH

KITCHEN SCIENCE

Nick Arnold

QEB

CONTENTS

INTRODUCTION   6

CHAPTER 1: MAD MIXTURES

Best ever butter   8
Solid liquid wonders   10
Sticky situations   12
Kitchen sunset   14
Giant candies   16
Salad dressing secrets   18

CHAPTER 2: FLOATING AND FORCES

Liquid layers   20
Floating fact-finder   22
Restless raisins   24
Kitchen bag challenge   26
Watery wonders   28
Sink or swim?   32
Whirling whirlpool   34
A smashing experiment!   36

CHAPTER 3: COLORFUL CHEMISTRY

Milky marvels   38
Quick-change act   40
Giant green egg   42
Foamy fun   46
Crazy lemon volcano   48

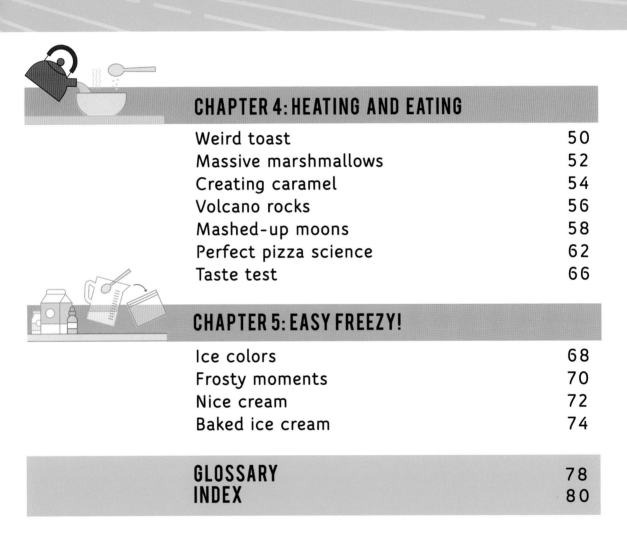

CHAPTER 4: HEATING AND EATING

Weird toast 50

Massive marshmallows 52

Creating caramel 54

Volcano rocks 56

Mashed-up moons 58

Perfect pizza science 62

Taste test 66

CHAPTER 5: EASY FREEZY!

Ice colors 68

Frosty moments 70

Nice cream 72

Baked ice cream 74

GLOSSARY 78

INDEX 80

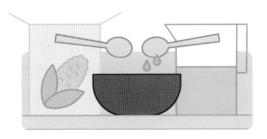

INTRODUCTION

Science is about everything. It's even about food and drink. That's why this book is called *Kitchen Science*. It's full of science experiments that you can try in your kitchen. And you even get to EAT some of your experiments! Here's what's on the menu...

CHAPTER 1:
MAD MIXTURES

is all about what happens when you mix or separate food and liquids.

CHAPTER 2:
FLOATING AND FORCES

looks at the forces in liquids and how air in your mixture affects the way it behaves.

CHAPTER 3:
COLORFUL CHEMISTRY

gets to grips with crucial kitchen chemicals such as detergents and acids.

CHAPTER 4:
HEATING AND EATING

checks out cooking chemistry and how heat changes food, and you'll find out about moons, microbes, and volcanoes, too!

CHAPTER 5:
EASY FREEZY!

proves that science doesn't stop when the temperature drops. Freezing can be fun, too!

Golden rules
FOR SENSIBLE SCIENTISTS

Rule 1
BE ORGANIZED

Before you start an experiment, read the instructions and make sure you have everything you need at hand.

Look out for the handy hints in circles—they will help to make the experiments work.

Rule 2
BE SAFE!

Ask for adult help wherever you see this symbol. Always follow the WARNING! advice in the red boxes. Never experiment with flames, mains electricity, or gas. Always ask an adult to do any cutting.

ASK AN ADULT

⚠ WARNING! Water may spill at stage 4.

Rule 3
BE TIDY!

Start and finish with a clean and tidy working area. Look out for the yellow MESS WARNING! boxes and follow the advice given.

⚠ MESS WARNING! Food coloring stains—wear old clothes!

You can try these experiments in any order, but the science explanations make more sense if you tackle them in the order they appear in this book. What's certain is that wherever you start, you're sure to get a taste for kitchen science!

READY — STEADY — EXPERIMENT!

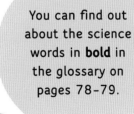

You can find out about the science words in **bold** in the glossary on pages 78–79.

BEST EVER BUTTER

This chapter is about mixing materials, but let's start by separating stuff. It's the secret of the best butter ever.

1 Cool the stand mixer bowl in the fridge for two hours.

2 Measure out 1 ¼ cup (280 ml) of heavy cream and pour it into the cold bowl. Add a pinch of salt if you like salty butter. Switch on the mixer. After about two minutes, the cream will thicken into whipped cream. Keep mixing! The cream will form soft lumps, then turn yellow and look like scrambled egg.

ASK AN ADULT

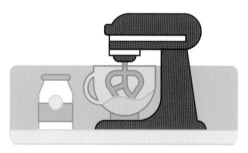

3 If any liquid appears, drain it off. Continue to mix until no more liquid appears.

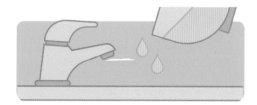

4 Wash your hands, then firmly squeeze the mixture to remove any remaining liquid. Pat the butter dry using tea towels.

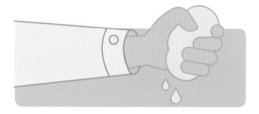

5 Shape the butter using the back of a teaspoon and place it in a container with a cover.

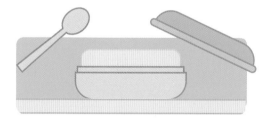

6 Enjoy your homemade butter on toast with your favorite jam. Or use it for the experiments on pages 50, 56, and 59.

You will need...

- Heavy cream
- Measuring cup
- Stand mixer
- Tea towels
- Covered container
- Tablespoon
- Salt (optional)

The Science:
FAT AND PROTEIN

Cream is made from microscopic droplets of fat in water. Each droplet has a thin coat made of **protein**.

Blending breaks open the protein coats. This allows the fat droplets to clump together and form butter. The leftover water and protein is called buttermilk. Some water is left in the butter, making it slightly soft and moist.

Store your butter in the fridge and use it within five days.

SOLID LIQUID WONDERS

Solids are dry and liquids are wet—simple, huh? But some substances can be both wet AND dry. Confused? It's all to do with mixing.

3 Swirl the mixture in the bowl and then run your fingers through it. Now try pressing down on the mixture. What do you notice?

1 Put two tablespoons of cornstarch into a bowl. Add one tablespoon of water and stir thoroughly.

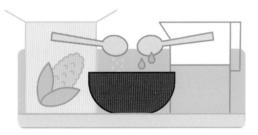

2 Stir in 10 drops of green food coloring. Add a few drops of water and stir again until the mixture is thick and smooth.

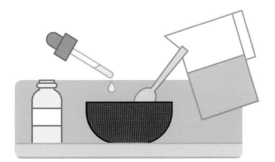

The food coloring isn't vital, but it makes the goo look more interesting— and gross!

The Science:
NON-NEWTONIAN FLUIDS

The mixture flows like a liquid, but when you touch it, WEIRDLY it feels solid. Scientists call this a "non-Newtonian fluid," after scientist Sir Isaac Newton (1642–1726), who studied the way liquids behave.

The gooey, mixed-up material flows like liquid because it consists of cornstarch grains floating in water. When you press the mixture with your fingers, you push away most of the water, making it feel solid.

The quality that makes a liquid thick or runny is called **viscosity**. A thick liquid is more viscous than a runny liquid because its **molecules** rub together more.

STICKY SITUATIONS

On their own, flour and water aren't sticky, so how can they make glue? *Stick* with this experiment to find out.

MESS WARNING!
This can be quite a messy experiment.
Wear old clothes!

1 Cut or tear some newspaper into 30 strips, each measuring about 1 x 8 inches (2.5 x 20 cm).

2 Pour some flour into a glass to a height of about 1 inch (2.5 cm), then tip the flour into a bowl. Do the same with about 1 inch (2.5 cm) of water.

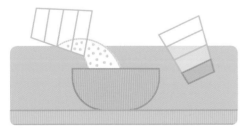

3 Stir the glue mixture until it is thick and creamy, and all the lumps have disappeared.

4 On the printer paper, cover an area 8 x 8 inches (20 x 20 cm) with glue. Lay three strips of newspaper as shown. Gently press the strips with the spoon so the glue soaks through the newspaper strips.

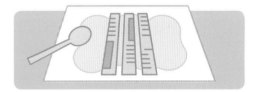

5 Spread some glue on top of the newspaper strips and place three more strips, as shown, pressing down gently.

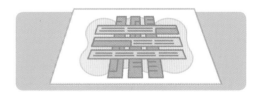

6 Repeat steps 4 and 5 until you've used up all your strips. Use paper towels to wipe any surplus glue from the edges of the paper. Leave the paper to dry for 24 hours in a warm place.

- Newspaper
- Bowl
- Spoon
- Glass
- Ruler
- Scissors
- Sheet of printer-size paper
- Plain flour
- Water
- Paper towels

7 Try to tear the printer paper in half. You should find it is impossible!

The Science: STARCH AND CELLULOSE

Wheat plants use starch to store food. So when wheat seeds are ground up to make flour, the flour contains microscopic grains of starch. The water soaks into the starch grains, which swell and burst, releasing tangled-up starch molecules.

Paper is made of fibers of a substance called cellulose, which is also made by plants. The starch and cellulose molecules tangle together to make a strong bond that sets hard, so the newspaper will not tear.

DID YOU KNOW?

Sticky starch molecules make sticky rice sticky when you cook it.

KITCHEN SUNSET

It's simple to make a sunset in your kitchen.
All you need is a magical milk mixture...

This experiment should take place in a darkened room—or after dark. The glass should hold at least 2 cups (480 ml) of water.

3 Place the glass between yourself and the flashlight so the light shines toward you through the water. Note the color of the mixture.

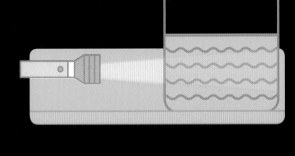

Fill a tall, straight-sided glass with 2 cups (480 ml) of water. Stir in two tablespoons of milk.

Point the flashlight down at the surface of the mixture and note its color.

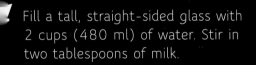

4 Hold the flashlight against the base of the glass and shine the light up through the water. Note the color of the mixture.

DID YOU KNOW?

Sunset and sunrise appear redder after a volcanic eruption because particles thrown into the air reflect away more blue light than normal.

The Science: SCATTERING LIGHT

Sunlight contains all the colors of the rainbow. As it shines through Earth's **atmosphere**, it hits trillions of air molecules. At midday, when the sun is overhead and has less atmosphere to travel through, blue light reflects strongly from and between the molecules, so the sky looks blue. At sunset, the sun shines at a low angle and sunlight passes through more of the Earth's atmosphere. Most of the blue light is reflected away, and you see red light, which doesn't reflect strongly from air molecules.

Some sunsets make the sky glow red due to reddish light reflecting off clouds.

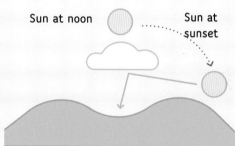

Sun at noon

Sun at sunset

Your experiment works in the same way. Milk molecules reflect blue light more strongly, so the milky water looks bluish from above. But when the light shines *through* the milk, the liquid looks yellower or even reddish, just like a sunset.

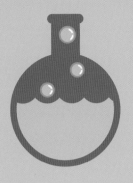

GIANT CANDIES

Believe it or not, you can make super-size candies in your own kitchen! Try it for yourself...

1 Put one candy in a glass of water and another on a plate. Put them both in the fridge.

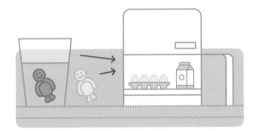

2 After 12 hours, compare the candies. Which candy is bigger? Record their sizes on paper.

3 Add a level dessert spoon of salt to a glass of warm water. Stir the mixture until all the salt has dissolved.

4 Put the biggest candy in the salty water and leave it for two hours. Then measure the size of both candies again. How has the larger candy changed size?

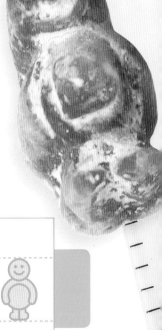

DID YOU KNOW?

Gummy candies contain gelatine, which is made from animal protein. It makes them firm and chewy.

You will need...

- Two gummy candies (like jelly babies or gummi bears)
- Glass
- Plate
- Salt
- Water
- Pencil
- Dessert spoon

Wash your hands before you begin this experiment.

0cm

1

2

5

The gummy candy that you don't put in water is there to help you compare the changes to the candy that does go in water. In an experiment, an item that is used like this to compare changes is called a "control."

The Science: DIFFUSION

Like all liquid or gas molecules, water molecules are constantly moving. A gummy candy contains gelatine, a jelly-like protein molecule. Gelatine has a structure where moving water molecules can squeeze in between the gelatine molecules by a process called diffusion and join with them. The additional water molecules that have joined to the gelatine molecules cause the gummy candy to swell in size and **mass**.

Placing a gummy candy in a salt solution allows salt particles to diffuse into the gelatine. Salt particles take the place of the water molecules joined to the gelatine molecules. The gummy candy loses water molecules and it shrinks to a smaller size.

SALAD DRESSING SECRETS

Salad dressing contains oil and vinegar—two substances that don't mix. So how can you stop them from separating?

1 Pour ¹⁄₃ cup (80 ml) of brown vinegar into a measuring jug.

3 Easy! Just add two teaspoons of mustard and stir well. Ta-da! You've made the substances mix together. See opposite to find out what's going on.

2 Add ¹⁄₂ cup (120 ml) of olive oil, bringing the liquid level to about 7 ounces (200 ml). Notice that the oil and vinegar don't mix—they separate into two separate layers, with the oil floating on top of the vinegar. What can you do to stop them separating so they make a salad dressing?

Salad dressing challenge

Say you put ¹⁄₂ cup (120 ml) of brown vinegar and ¹⁄₂ cup (120 ml) of olive oil into the measuring cup by mistake. How can you correct the quantities to ¹⁄₃ and ¹⁄₂ cup (80/120 ml)? Clue: you'll need a funnel and a screw-top bottle.

Answer:
Pour the oil and vinegar into the bottle using the funnel. Tighten the screw top and hold the bottle upside down until the liquids separate. Keeping the bottle upside down, hold it over the measuring cup and loosen the top just enough to allow 1¹⁄₂ ounces (40 ml) of vinegar to dribble into the cup. Tighten the top again. The bottle will now contain the correct quantities of oil and vinegar.

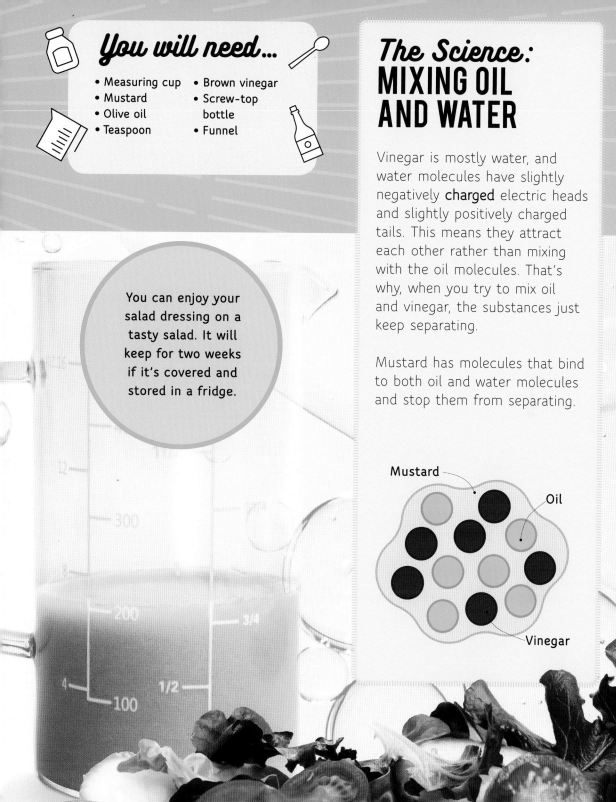

You will need...

- Measuring cup
- Mustard
- Olive oil
- Teaspoon
- Brown vinegar
- Screw-top bottle
- Funnel

The Science:
MIXING OIL AND WATER

Vinegar is mostly water, and water molecules have slightly negatively **charged** electric heads and slightly positively charged tails. This means they attract each other rather than mixing with the oil molecules. That's why, when you try to mix oil and vinegar, the substances just keep separating.

Mustard has molecules that bind to both oil and water molecules and stop them from separating.

You can enjoy your salad dressing on a tasty salad. It will keep for two weeks if it's covered and stored in a fridge.

Mustard

Oil

Vinegar

CHAPTER 2: FLOATING AND FORCES
LIQUID LAYERS

Your kitchen is full of forces that are hard at work. In this experiment, discover an awesome balance of forces that makes things float or sink.

 MESS WARNING!
Food coloring stains—wear old clothes!

1 Add a few drops of food coloring to a small glass of water to make a nice strong color. Stir the mixture.

2 Pour ½ inch (1.2 cm) of golden syrup into a tall glass. Then add ½ inch (1.2 cm) of glycerine, ½ inch (1.2 cm) of colored water, and ½ inch (1.2 cm) of olive oil. The liquids will separate into layers.

3 Carefully put a split pea onto the surface of the olive oil.

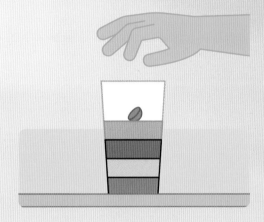

4 Time how long it takes the split pea to sink through each layer of liquid. What do you notice?

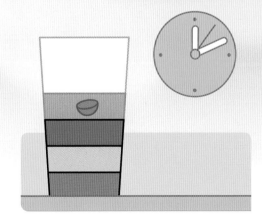

You will need...

- Glycerine
- Food coloring
- Golden syrup
- Split peas
- Tall glass
- Small glass
- Teaspoon
- Olive oil
- Ruler
- Watch with a second hand

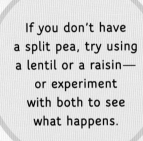

If you don't have a split pea, try using a lentil or a raisin— or experiment with both to see what happens.

The Science: FLOATING AND DENSITY

This experiment has several floating liquid layers. Each layer floats because it's less **dense** than the layer underneath.

Denser substances contain more matter for their volume than less dense substances. They also push back harder when you press on them. Your split pea sank more slowly through the denser liquid layers because these layers pushed back harder than the less dense layers.

The force of a liquid pushing up is called upthrust. When the split pea settles on a layer, the upthrust force exactly balances the weight of the split pea. The speed at which the pea falls through a layer depends on the density of the liquid and how viscous (thick) the liquid is.

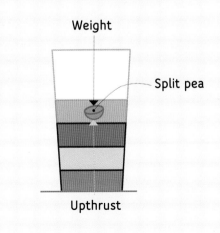

Weight

Split pea

Upthrust

FLOATING FACT-FINDER

You don't need fancy science equipment to measure the density of liquids. All you need is a drinking straw and some adhesive putty!

1 Fill two glasses with warm water to within 1 inch (2.5 cm) of the top.

2 Stir 5 teaspoons of salt into one glass. Stir the mixture until all the salt has dissolved. Fill the third glass with cooking oil to within 1 inch (2.5 cm) of the top.

3 Cut a 2-inch (5 cm) length of drinking straw. Make a ball of adhesive putty about $\frac{1}{2}$ inch (1.2 cm) across and mold it over and around the end of the straw so that it blocks the hole.

4 Place the straw upright in the fresh water, putty-end down. Use a waterproof marker to mark the water level on the straw. Now put the straw into the salty water and mark the water level again.

The Science:
FLOATING AND SINKING

You've made a hydrometer! This instrument measures how dense a liquid is compared with water.

Imagine you're swimming. Your weight pulls you down into the water, but the force of upthrust pushes you up (see page 21).

You will need...

- Three identical small glasses
- Cooking oil
- Adhesive putty
- Drinking straws
- Ruler
- Salt
- Teaspoon
- Waterproof marker

5 Finally, put the straw upright into the cooking oil. Mark the oil level on the straw. Does it float higher or lower than in the fresh water?

The two forces are roughly equal, which is why it's quite hard to sink to the bottom of a swimming pool.

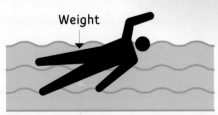

Weight

Upthrust

Dense liquids have greater upthrust, which means objects float higher in them. Salty water is denser than fresh water and has greater upthrust, so your hydrometer floats higher in salty water. Cooking oil is less dense than fresh water, so its upthrust is weaker and your hydrometer floats lower. Do you think it would be easier or harder to swim in cooking oil?

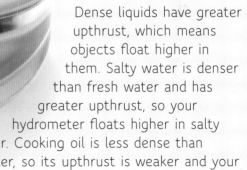

RESTLESS RAISINS

Raisins don't take swimming lessons, but they are great swimmers! Try this experiment to see them in action...

1 Pour a glass of lemon-lime soda.

2 Add 10 raisins to the glass.

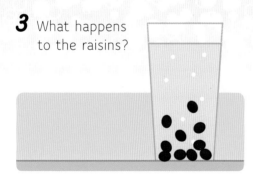

3 What happens to the raisins?

4 Now fill a screw-top jar with soda and add 10 raisins. Close the lid and give the jar a shake.

Use soda from a new bottle that hasn't been opened before.

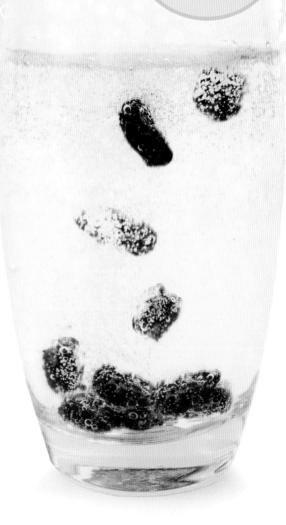

You will need...

- Screw-top jar
- Tall glass
- Raisins
- Fizzy lemon-lime soda
- Tablespoon

The Science:
FLOATING AND BUOYANCY

An object's weight acts downward, and when in a liquid, an upthrust force acts upward on it (see pages 21 and 23). In fact, any object floats if the weight of liquid it pushes aside is equal to its own weight. The ability to float is called "buoyancy."

When you add raisins to the soda, they sink because they're heavier than the soda they push aside.

But like any fizzy drink, lemon-lime soda contains dissolved **carbon dioxide** gas. In the bottle, the gas doesn't form bubbles because the liquid is under pressure. When you open the bottle, you release the pressure and bubbles of gas appear.

When you add the raisins, bubbles form on the rough surface of the raisins. The gas bubbles make the raisins lighter than the volume of soda they are pushing aside, so the raisins rise to the surface. Then the bubbles burst, making the raisins heavier, so they sink.

In step 5, the raisins in the jar became less active after a few minutes because, 1) after you released some of the gas, there was less gas to make bubbles; and 2) with the lid on, the pressure on the remaining bubbles stopped them from growing big enough to raise the raisins.

5 Loosen the lid to release some of the gas, then tighten it so that no more gas can escape. Watch the raisins for a few minutes. Which raisins were most active, those in the jar or those in the glass? Check out The Science (right) to find out why the raisins behaved differently.

KITCHEN BAG CHALLENGE

Getting a bag out of a jar should be easy, right? So why is this task impossible? Blame the air!

1 Take a plastic bag, put it over the top of a glass jar, and secure it with wide clear tape or masking tape. Pull the tape tight to make an airtight seal.

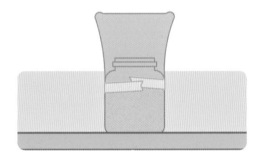

2 Try to push the bag into the jar. Sounds easy? But it really isn't! OK, remove the bag and tape from the jar.

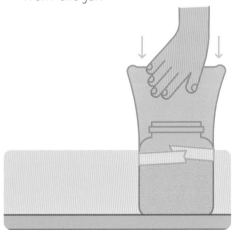

3 Now place the plastic bag inside the jar and fold the top down over the outside of the jar. Wrap sticky tape tightly around the bag to secure it.

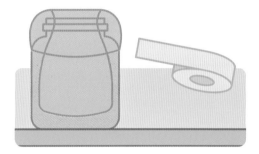

4 Now try to pull the bag out from inside the jar. What happens?

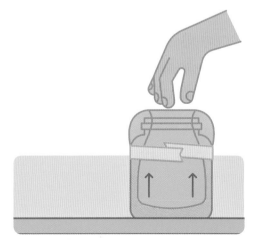

- Scissors
- Clean plastic food bag
- Wide clear tape or masking tape

The Science:
AIR PRESSURE

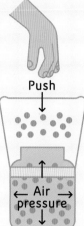

In step 1, the jar appears to be empty, but actually it's full of air molecules. When you try to push the bag into the jar, the air molecules are squashed together. The harder you push, the harder the air molecules push back. It's impossible to push the bag into the jar! The force of air pressing on a surface is called air pressure.

Push

← Air → pressure

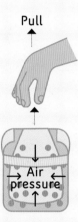

When you try to pull the bag out of the jar, you're fighting against air pressure pressing on the bag. The force of the air pressure is so strong that it's impossible to pull the bag out from the jar.

Pull

Air ← pressure

DID YOU KNOW?

Air pressure is amazingly strong. In fact, the air pressure on your head is equal to carrying around a small car! Your body can withstand the pressure, and you don't notice it because it's always there.

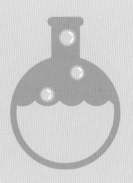

WATERY WONDERS

Water isn't colorless and boring—it's got hidden depths. You can even make it do tricks without getting your hands wet!

MESS WARNING!
Water will probably get spilled in this experiment! Have paper towels and tea towels handy for cleanup operations!

WARNING!
Wet glass can be slippery—hold the jars firmly.

1 Fill the plastic tub with water. Hold both jars completely underwater at an angle on their sides so that all the air escapes from inside them.

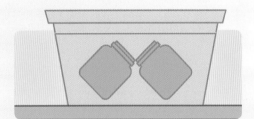

2 Bring the jars together, rim to rim, under the water.

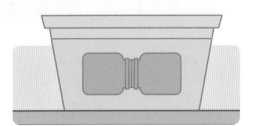

3 Still holding the two jars together, carefully lift them from the bowl. Stand the two jars on the tray as shown. Try not to spill any water. Dry your hands.

4 Holding the lower jar steady, slide the upper jar a tiny bit to one side to leave a very small gap. You may need help to do this.

ASK AN ADULT

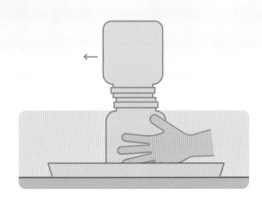

You will need...

- Large plastic tub
- Cotton cloth or tea towel
- Drinking straw
- Water
- Two identical glass jars
- Large tray with high sides
- Ribbon or rubber band
- Glass

5 Hold the drinking straw so it points at the small gap between the jars. The end of the straw should be about $1/2$ inch (1.2 cm) away from the gap. Blow gently through the drinking straw. What happens?

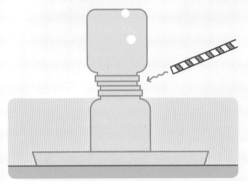

6 Now for a different trick! Fill one of the jars to the brim with water and cover it with a cotton cloth. The water may soak through the fabric. Tie a ribbon tightly around the top of the jar so the fabric can't move at all.

7 Gently turn the jar upside down. What happens this time?

If you don't have a large plastic tub, any large bowl will do. Instead of a tray, you could use a roasting dish.

The Science:
SURFACE TENSION

Because water molecules are drawn together (see page 19), the surface of water acts like a thin, stretchy skin. This is called "surface tension." The stretchy skin allows water to form into drops. It is even strong enough for some insects and spiders to walk on it.

Using the straw you can blow air with enough force to break through the surface tension. The air forms bubbles. The bubbles float up and merge to form an air space with enough air pressure to push water from the top jar. If you blow enough air into the water, you can empty all the water from the top jar without touching the jars!

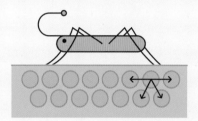

As you pull the two jars slightly apart, surface tension stops the water from leaking out. But surface tension isn't very strong. If you move the jars too far apart, you will break the surface tension and water will leak from the gap between the jars.

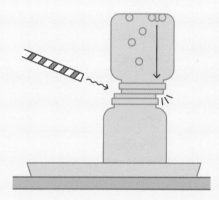

Steps 7 and 8 once more show surface tension in action. Like paper (see page 13), cotton consists of cellulose fibers. Water molecules are attracted to the fibers. Surface tension makes water push upward between the fibers, but stops it from escaping from the fabric. This is why the water doesn't pour out when you turn the jar upside down.

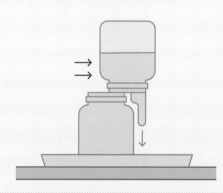

DID YOU KNOW?

On Earth you rarely find round drops of water because air resistance distorts them. But in space, where air resistance is weaker, surface tension pulls a drop into a perfectly round ball.

Watery wonder challenges:
CAN YOU FIGURE THEM OUT?

1 Fill a glass with water and lower a paper clip onto the water surface end-on. Now lay another paper clip flat on the water's surface. Why does one paper clip sink and the other float? Clue: look at the surface through a magnifying glass and think of the paper clip's weight pressing on the water's surface.

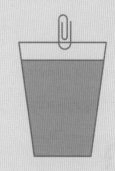

2 Very carefully pour some water into a glass until it reaches the very top. Look at the surface closely. Why does the water bulge above the rim of the glass?

Answer 1:

Surface tension supports the paper clip when you lay it flat on the water, but it's not strong enough to bear the weight of the end-on paper clip.

Answer 2:

As the water reaches the top of the glass, surface tension tries to stop it from spilling over the rim. Instead the water's surface bulges upward.

31

SINK OR SWIM?

Two balls of paper go for a swim.
One ball sadly sinks and the other
surprisingly swims, but why?

1 Draw and cut out two paper
squares measuring about
1 x 1 inch (2.5 x 2.5 cm).

2 Screw each piece of paper
into a ball about ³/₄ inch
(2 cm) across.

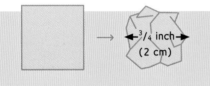

³/₄ inch
(2 cm)

3 Fill two identical glasses
with exactly the same
amount of water.

4 Gently dribble a tablespoon
of dishwashing liquid into the
water in one of the glasses.

This is a comparison
experiment. By using two
glasses of water that are
identical except for the
dishwashing liquid, you know
it must be the dishwashing
liquid that affects
the result.

5 Using a hand whisk, gently swirl the water. Try not to make bubbles or spill any water. The water will take on the color of the dishwashing liquid.

6 Lower a paper ball into each glass of water. What happens to the paper balls? Find out why in the box below.

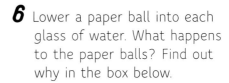

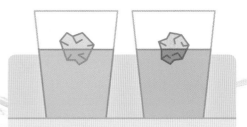

The Science:
DETERGENT AND WATER TENSION

You might think that the water would soak into both paper balls equally, increasing their density and making them sink to the bottom of the glasses. But the ball in fresh water floats! Surface tension between the water molecules holds them together and slows down the water from seeping into the cracks in the paper ball.

Dishwashing liquid contains detergent molecules. One end of a molecule of detergent pulls on a molecule of water. The detergent molecule tugs the water molecule away from the other water molecules. This breaks the surface tension around the paper ball, so the water soaks into the cracks until it's dense enough to sink.

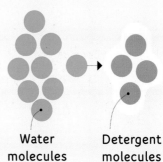

Water molecules   Detergent molecules

WHIRLING WHIRLPOOL

Whirling whirlpools suck people to a watery doom.
You can make a miniature whirlpool of your own,
but don't panic! Yours will be locked in a bottle.

1 Fill a measuring cup with water.
Pour the water into a plastic bottle
until it is three-quarters full.

2 Add four drops
of food coloring.
Put the lid on
the bottle and
shake to mix.

3 Remove the lid of the bottle and
add enough olive oil to make a
layer $\frac{1}{2}$ inch (1.2 cm) thick.

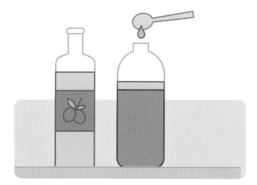

4 Put the lid back on tight.
Hold the sides of the bottle
and move it in circles as
fast as you can.
Look for your
whirlpool!

DID YOU KNOW?

Vortices (more than one vortex)
are spinning masses of air or
water, and they are surprisingly
common. You'll find them:

• In tornadoes, which are
violent air vortices

• Behind the wings of a plane
as it flies through the air

• In storms on other planets,
such as the Great Red Spot
on the planet Jupiter

• In a bathtub, as water goes
down the drain

You will need...

- Olive oil
- Ruler
- Measuring cup
- Liquid food coloring or glitter
- Tablespoon
- 16.9-ounce (500 ml) plastic or glass bottle with screw cap or cork
- Water

If you need to remove any labels from the bottle, ask an adult to soak it in hot, soapy water and then scrub them off.

5 Put the bottle down and watch what happens to the oil.

The Science: A VORTEX

Your miniature whirlpool is a spinning funnel, or vortex, of oil that forms in the water.

Swirling the bottle around causes the water and oil to spin in the bottle. Water is denser than olive oil and is thrown toward the sides of the bottle. Olive oil and air fill in the space in the middle of the water, forming a vortex.

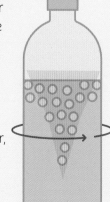

A SMASHING EXPERIMENT!

Here's how to freak out your friends with an amazing trick and NOT get grounded for smashing the best china!

> **MESS WARNING!**
> Your plastic plates, bowls or glasses may fall to the floor, so put a cushion under the edge of the table to stop them from breaking.

1 Completely clear the table. Place a large sheet of shiny wrapping paper on the table like a tablecloth.

2 On the wrapping paper, set the table for two people with plastic cups, plates or bowls, and spoons.

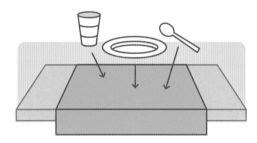

3 Put a mandarin on/in each plastic plate or bowl and in each cup.

4 Stand at arm's length from the table. Pinch the wrapping paper and gently pull it toward you. What happens?

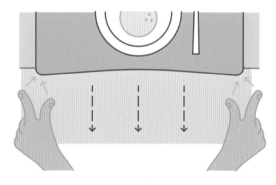

5 Now pull the wrapping paper as fast and smoothly as you can. It should come right out from under the plates or bowls, spoons, and cups, leaving them standing!

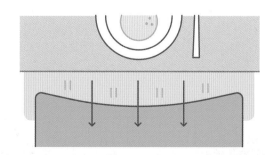

It's a good idea to practice this experiment several times before you perform it in front of your friends and family!

The Science: INERTIA

Sir Isaac Newton's First Law of Motion says that an object will stay still or move in a straight line until an unbalanced force acts on it. The quality that makes an object do this is called **inertia**.

When you pull the wrapping paper gently, a rubbing force called **friction** keeps the objects on the wrapping paper. They move with the paper. But the force of friction between the objects and the wrapping paper is quite weak.

When you pull the paper quickly, the force of your pull overcomes the force of friction. You're able to pull the wrapping paper off the table, but the inertia of the plates or bowls, spoons, and cups keeps them where they were.

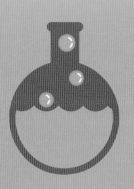

MILKY MARVELS

Kitchen science is all about chemistry, and it can get pretty colourful! Have fun making bright, swirling patterns and discover why they happen.

MESS WARNING!
Food coloring stains—
wear old clothes!

1 Pour just enough milk into a bowl to cover the bottom.

2 Pour a blob of dishwashing liquid onto a saucer. Roll one end of a cotton swab in the dishwashing liquid.

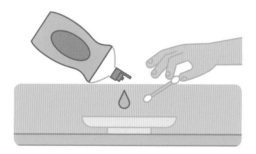

3 Use a paintbrush to add 2-3 drops of food coloring to the milk. The color may start to merge with the milk.

4 Quickly touch the milk with the end of the cotton swab that you dipped in the dishwashing liquid.

5 Repeat steps 3 and 4 using different shades of food coloring. Have fun making lots of swirling patterns.

Try this experiment several times. You might like to photograph your results! Try using different kinds of milk, or milk at different temperatures. Which combination of milk and temperature gives the best results?

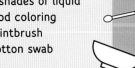

You will need...

- Shallow bowl or dish
- Saucer
- 2% milk
- Dishwashing liquid
- 3 shades of liquid food coloring
- Paintbrush
- Cotton swab

The Science:
SWIRLING LIQUIDS AND MIXING

The colors swirl out across the milk, but why? Milk consists of fat, protein, and vitamin molecules floating in water. The water in milk has surface tension, just like fresh water.

Dishwashing liquid is a detergent, and as you found out on page 33, one end of a detergent molecule grabs a water molecule. This breaks the surface tension of water. But detergent molecules have another trick up their sleeve. The other end of the detergent molecule grabs a fat molecule.

When you add the dishwashing liquid, the detergent molecules break the surface tension of the milk and create currents in it. As the water and food coloring molecules are pushed aside, the colours form swirling patterns.

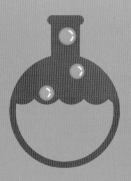

QUICK-CHANGE ACT

How can you make a liquid change color in your kitchen? All you need is a little chemistry...

1 Add ¹/₂ cup (120 ml) of red grape juice to each glass.

2 Add two teaspoons of baking soda to one of the glasses and stir well.

3 Compare the colors of the liquids. What has happened?

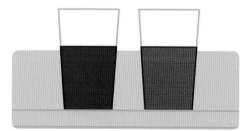

The Science:
ACIDS, BASES, INDICATORS, AND COLORS

Grape juice contains an acid chemical. When you combine a strong acid with water, the acid dissolves other substances. Luckily the acid in grape juice isn't strong enough to harm you! Baking soda is a weak **alkali**—an alkali is a type of **base** that dissolves in water. A strong alkali dissolved in water can dissolve other substances in a similar way to acids.

The alkali in the baking soda is strong enough to alter color molecules in the grape juice. As the molecules change, they reflect different colors of light. The liquid appears to change color to a dark blue-purple.

At the same time, bubbles appear. These are carbon dioxide gas bubbles produced by a **chemical reaction** between the alkaline baking soda and the acid in the grape juice.

Scientists measure how acidic a substance is using the pH scale. The lower the pH of a substance, the more acidic it is. Alkalis have a higher pH. A substance such as grape juice that changes color according to pH is called an indicator.

DID YOU KNOW?

Acids have a sour taste. The sour taste of lemon and vinegar are due to the acids they contain.

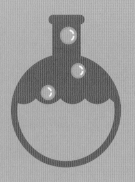

GIANT GREEN EGG

With just a little chemistry magic, you can turn a normal egg into a giant green egg—no giant green chickens involved! Turn the page to see the egg-stra-ordinary green egg.

1 Gently place an egg into a glass. Pour $^2/_3$ cup (160 ml) of white, cider, or white wine vinegar over the egg.

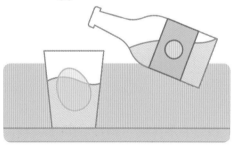

Turn the egg a few times in the vinegar so that the liquid is in contact with all areas of the eggshell.

2 Rest a dessert spoon on the egg to stop it from floating and leave it in the vinegar for 24 hours, turning it occasionally. What happens to the egg?

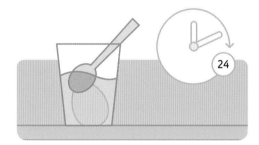

3 Take the egg out of the vinegar, gently dry it with a paper towel, and drop it into the sink from a height of 1 $^1/_2$ to 2 inches (4 to 5 cm) cm. What happens?

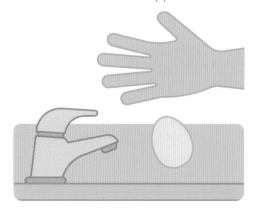

You will need...

- Egg
- Glass
- Measuring cup
- Two glass jars, 2 to 3 times bigger than the egg
- Green food coloring
- Saucer
- Sugar
- White, cider, or white wine vinegar
- Dessert spoon
- Pencil
- Paper towel
- Water
- Cling film
- Flashlight

4 Take a glass jar two to three times bigger than the egg. Cover the bottom of the jar with sugar. Place the egg on the sugar and pour on more sugar until the egg is just covered.

5 Leave the egg in the sugar for a further 36 hours.

36

6 Carefully remove the egg and place it in a saucer. Gently press it with the blunt end of a pencil. What happens?

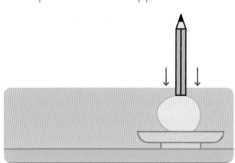

7 Take a clean glass jar and pour in some water. Add enough green food coloring to turn the water a strong, dark green.

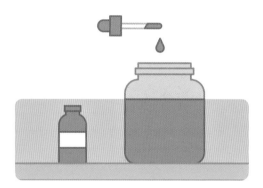

8 Gently wash the egg and place it in the green water. Leave it for 24 hours. Then, use the spoon to gently remove the egg from the water and place it on a saucer. How has the egg changed?

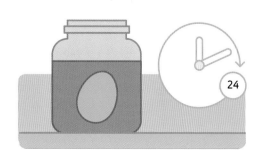

24

43

DID YOU KNOW?

Vinegar is at least 4 percent acetic acid. Bacteria feeding on alcohol or sugars makes the acid.

Try experimenting with other food colors. It's possible to make giant red, yellow, and blue eggs, too!

The Science:
ACIDS AND OSMOSIS

This experiment combines two ways in which materials change—dissolving and osmosis.

Vinegar contains acid, and eggshells are mostly chalk, also known as calcium carbonate. The acid in the vinegar dissolves the calcium carbonate. The bubbles you see in step 2 are carbon dioxide gas produced by this chemical reaction.

After 24 hours, the eggshell has dissolved, leaving behind the rubbery inner layer of the egg. Because the surface is now rubbery, the egg bounces when you drop it!

Some chemical reactions can be reversed, but others, such as dissolving calcium carbonate, can't. Once you've dissolved the eggshell, you can't get it back!

After 36 hours in the sugar, the egg feels soft and saggy. You can make a dent in it if you gently press it with a pencil. Eggshells protect an egg from losing water, but without its shell, the egg loses water into the sugar by osmosis, leaving it saggy. The water that has come out of the egg turns the sugar into a gloopy syrup.

Thanks to the sugar, there isn't much water left in the egg. So when you place the egg in colored water, water soaks into it by osmosis and the egg swells to become a giant egg. Color molecules pass into the egg too, turning it green!

Egg challenge:
CAN YOU MAKE AN EGG GLOW IN THE DARK?

Take another egg and soak it in vinegar for 24 hours to dissolve its shell. You'll now be able to shine a light through it! Wait until dark, then set up the display as shown. The egg will appear to glow in the dark!

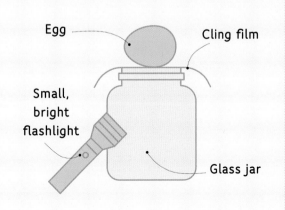

Egg

Cling film

Small, bright flashlight

Glass jar

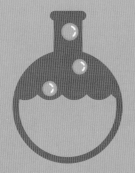

FOAMY FUN

If there's one thing better than bubbles, it's LOADS OF BUBBLES. And if there's one thing better than loads of bubbles, it's LOADS OF COLORED BUBBLES! Here's how to make them.

 MESS WARNING!
Food coloring stains fabrics. Put down newspaper and keep food coloring away from curtains and carpets.

 WARNING!
If you have sensitive skin, try bubble bath instead of dishwashing liquid.

1 Measure ½ cup (120 ml) of water into a large bowl. Add two tablespoons of dishwashing liquid.

2 Add 10 drops of food coloring (all one color) to the mixture.

3 **ASK AN ADULT** Ask an adult to blend the mixture for 2 minutes or until the foam can be pushed into peaks. They can use either a powerful handheld blender or a food processor.

4 **ASK AN ADULT** If your helper used a food processor, ask them to pour the bubble mixture back into the large bowl. Tip the large bowl as shown so the foam stays on one side of the bowl.

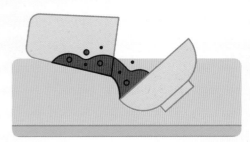

5 Repeat steps 1–4 using different food colorings. Try to keep the colored foam in separate segments in the bowl.

6 Now have fun swirling and mixing the colored foams. Notice how the colors change as you mix them.

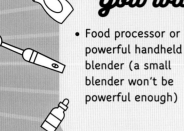

You will need...

- Food processor or powerful handheld blender (a small blender won't be powerful enough)
- Concentrated dishwashing liquid
- 3 or 4 shades of liquid food coloring, ideally red, green, and blue
- Water
- Tablespoon
- Large bowl
- Measuring cup

The Science:
MIXING BUBBLES AND COLORS

Water bubbles burst quickly because surface tension is always pulling the water molecules together, and away from air. But dishwashing liquid contains detergent molecules. Since one end of a detergent molecule grabs a water molecule (see page 33), you can mix detergent and water in thin layers. The layers surround trapped air to make longer-lasting bubbles!

When you mix different colors of foam, you might think the foam would get darker, but it actually gets paler. That's because the colors in the foam are really colored light reflecting from color molecules. Just like sunlight (see page 15), white light is a mixture of all colors. So the more colors you mix, the whiter the foam appears.

The different colors will show up best under a bright light.

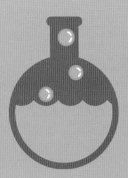

CRAZY LEMON VOLCANO

Want to turn a simple lemon into a mad, multi-colored volcano? Some colorful, chaotic chemistry can make that happen!

1 Ask an adult to cut a lemon in half. Place one half, cut side facing up, onto a sheet of black paper. Keep the other half for step 6.

ASK AN ADULT

2 Use the pointed end of a pencil to make holes $\frac{1}{2}$ inch (1.2 cm) deep around the edge of the cut surface of the lemon.

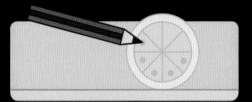

3 Put some water in a bowl. With a paintbrush, fill each hole with food coloring. Wash the brush in the water after each color.

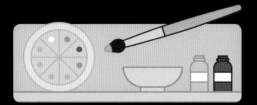

4 Pour a teaspoon of dishwashing liquid over the lemon flesh.

5 Sprinkle a few teaspoons of baking soda onto the cut lemon. Prod the flesh with the pencil.

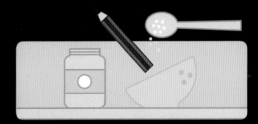

6 Squeeze a few drops of juice from the other half of the lemon onto the baking soda. Stand by for the eruption!

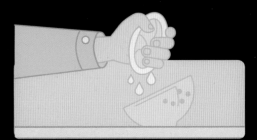

You will need...

- Lemon
- Knife
- Pencil
- Water
- Bowl
- Watercolor paintbrush
- Liquid food coloring
  (as many colors as you like)
- Dishwashing liquid
- 2 teaspoons
- Black paper
- Lemon juice
- Baking soda

Use ordinary dishwashing liquid rather than concentrated. If you only have concentrated, mix some water with it before you use it.

The Science:
ACID AND ALKALINE

Lemon juice contains acid—usually about 6 percent citric acid—and baking soda is an alkali (see page 41). When you mix an acid and an alkali, you trigger a chemical reaction that produces **neutral** substances, in this case water, a salt called sodium citrate, and carbon dioxide gas. A similar chemical reaction made carbon dioxide gas bubbles on an eggshell (page 42, step 2).

Mix detergent with water and air, and you make lots of bubbles. In this case the bubbles contain carbon dioxide gas, and the colors come from the food coloring!

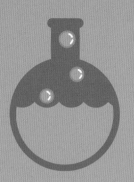

WEIRD TOAST

The previous chapter was all about chemistry without heat, but most kitchen chemistry uses heat—it's called cooking! Find out how to cook a simple piece of toast with a difference!

For your shape, instead of a toy figure you could use a cookie cutter or thick cardstock cut into whatever shape you want.

1 Take a slice of white bread and wrap it tightly in cling film.

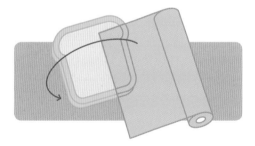

2 Press a toy figure or other shape into the bread. Press as hard as you can so the shape leaves a deep impression in the bread.

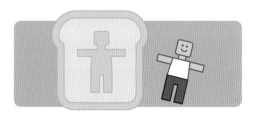

3 Remove the cling film. Ask an adult to set the toaster to its maximum setting, then toast the bread in the toaster.

ASK AN ADULT

4 Your shape should show clearly on the toast—and now you can eat it!

Bread browning challenge:
DESIGN A MOLD

Can you make a bread design using toy building blocks? Arrange the blocks in a pattern on a plate. Press the cling film wrapped bread firmly onto the blocks, unwrap, then get toasting!

You will need...

- Small toy figure
- Toaster
- Soft, white sliced bread
- Cling film

The Science:
INFRARED LIGHT AND BROWNING

Inside your toaster, bread is blasted with a type of light called infrared light. You can't see infrared light, but you can feel it. On a sunny day, your skin feels warm due to infrared rays from the sun warming it up.

When anything heats up, its molecules have more energy and try to move around. Heat can also speed up chemical reactions, and that's what happens when you toast bread. Bread contains starch and protein. All starch and protein molecules are made up of smaller molecules. Starch is made of sugar molecules and protein is made of amino acids. The heat from the toaster triggers a chemical reaction on the surface of the bread between sugars and amino acids. This chemical reaction is called "browning." It results in the brown color and scent molecules that make a toasty smell.

The pressed areas appear paler because the pressed surface is smooth. The normally rough bits of bread dry out and become hotter than the smooth bits. The rough bits therefore brown more quickly.

If you heat your toast too much, it turns black as starch sugars combine with oxygen gas from the air. The black bits contain lumps of carbon.

DID YOU KNOW?

Many foods, such as potatoes, meat, and coffee, turn brown when you roast them. This is due to a chemical reaction called "browning."

MASSIVE MARSHMALLOWS

Did you know you can make a normal marshmallow grow to twice its normal size? Here's how you do it!

> **WARNING!**
> Microwaved marshmallows get VERY HOT inside. Do NOT try to eat one until it has cooled!

1 See how far you can stretch a marshmallow without breaking it. Measure the length of the stretched marshmallow.

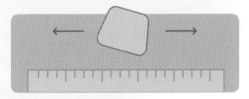

2 Fold one paper towel in four and put it on a plate. Place a marshmallow (not the stretched one!) on the paper towel. Ask an adult to microwave it for 40 seconds. Stand back and watch it through the window to see what happens.

ASK AN ADULT

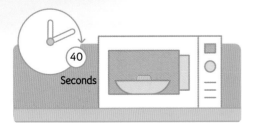

3 Allow the cooked marshmallow to cool for two minutes. What happens to it as it cools? Measure the height and width of the cooked marshmallow and an uncooked one. Write down the figures.

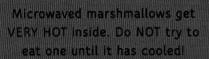

You will need...

- Plate
- Microwave oven
- Marshmallows
- Ruler
- Notebook and pencil
- Paper towel

Marshmallows are soft, light, and fluffy because they contain lots of tiny air bubbles. At least 50 percent of a marshmallow is air!

You can stretch unheated marshmallows because they contain a substance made from gelatine (see page 17). Gelatine is very stretchy.

As a marshmallow gets hotter, it gets larger. Inside the bubbles, heated air molecules push outward more strongly. As the bubbles grow, the sweets swell. The hot marshmallow also starts to melt, because heat weakens the bonds linking the molecules in the gelatine and sugar.

The heat kick-starts a chemical reaction called "caramelization." Like browning (see page 51), caramelization makes food brown and tasty, but this time the reaction breaks down sugar molecules and releases water. After two minutes in the microwave, the marshmallow will start to caramelize and turn brown.

4 Ask an adult to place another marshmallow in the microwave, this time for two minutes. How does this marshmallow compare to an uncooked one?

ASK AN ADULT

2

CREATING CARAMEL

Take some sugar, add a bit of kitchen chemistry, and make your very own yummy caramel. What's not to like?

1 Pour half a tablespoon of oil into the saucepan and smear it around with a paper towel.

2 Measure $1/4$ cup (50 g) of white sugar and put it in the saucepan.

3 Add two tablespoons of water and 4–5 drops of lemon juice.

4 Pour a little over 1.5 ounces (50 ml) of heavy cream into a measuring cup.

5 Ask an adult to heat the sugar mixture, moving the pan so that the mixture swirls around and heats evenly. The mixture needs to boil until it turns brown.

ASK AN ADULT

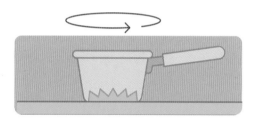

6 Once the mixture is a dark, sweet-smelling amber color, ask an adult to pour in the cream and briefly stir the mixture.

ASK AN ADULT

7 The adult should then remove the pan from the heat. When the mixture is cool, spread it on some bread or try it with ice cream—mmm!

ASK AN ADULT

Hot sugar sticks to things. Ask an adult to boil some water and pour it over every item that needs cleaning. This will loosen the sugar.

The Science:
EVAPORATION, CARAMELIZATION, AND CRYSTALS

As you heat the sugar and water, some of the water forms a gas called water vapor. This process is called **evaporation**. Water exists as solid ice, liquid water, and water vapor. What form you get depends on how hot or cold the water is.

Heating also turns the sugar from a solid into a liquid. The caramelization chemical reaction (see page 53) then turns the sugar a lovely brown color. You wiped the saucepan with oil and added lemon juice to the mixture to stop sugar **crystals** forming in the caramel and making it gritty.

DID YOU KNOW?

Dark caramel gives gravies and cola drinks a rich brown color.

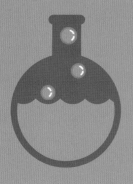

VOLCANO ROCKS

Have fun bubbling up some edible volcanic rock without blowing up your kitchen or filling your home with hot ash...

WARNING!
This is a hot sugar experiment. Keep clear of the hot mixture and do NOT eat it before it has cooled!

1 Put a little margarine or butter on a paper towel and wipe it over a baking tray.

2 Add ¾ cup (150 g) of caster sugar to a saucepan. Add four tablespoons of golden syrup. Ask an adult to heat the mixture gently and stir it until the sugar melts.

ASK AN ADULT

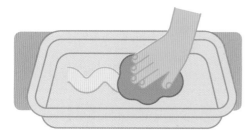

3 Let the mixture boil until it starts to darken. Ask an adult to take the saucepan off the heat and stir in two teaspoons of baking soda. What happens to the mixture?

ASK AN ADULT

4 Taking care to avoid spills, your adult helper should pour the mixture onto the baking tray. Allow the mixture to cool. Before you break it into bite-size pieces, what do you notice about the way it looks?

ASK AN ADULT

DID YOU KNOW?

Baking soda is found naturally in natron, the mineral used to preserve Egyptian mummies. It's also used to treat indigestion.

You will need...

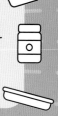

- Caster sugar
- Kitchen scales
- Tablespoon
- Golden syrup

- Deep saucepan
- Wooden spoon
- Baking soda
- Teaspoon

- Baking tray
- Margarine or butter
- Paper towel

The Science:
BAKING SODA AND VOLCANOES

When you added baking soda, it made the mixture bubble madly. The bubbles contain carbon dioxide gas.

Baking soda is an alkali, and you normally need to mix it with an acid to make carbon dioxide gas (see page 49). But in this experiment, the heat breaks up the baking soda molecules to produce carbon dioxide gas without any need for an acid.

The carbon dioxide gas bubbles get trapped in the cooling mixture and look just like the bubbles in some volcanic rocks. In volcanic rocks, the bubbles are formed by dissolved gas and steam when the rock is still hot and molten. Molten rock that has erupted from a volcano is called "lava."

MASHED-UP MOONS

Here's how to make your very own alien moons using mashed potato. Smashing!

Although the instructions are for four potato balls you can make as many as you like!

1 Wash your hands. Grease the baking tray with a little butter—this will help to stop the moons from sticking to the tray.

2 Put ¹/₄ cup (about 50 g) of instant potato mixture into a bowl. Your adult helper should then add just enough boiling water to make a firm mixture.

ASK AN ADULT

3 Stir the mashed potato—it should be a little drier than you would make it if you were eating it as mash. Leave it to cool for 30 minutes.

WARNING!
Mashed potato gets very hot. Let it cool before you shape it!

4 Roll the mash into four firm potato balls, or moons, about 3 inches (7.5 cm) across. Fill a glass with water and dip the teaspoon into it. Smooth the potato balls with the back of the wet teaspoon.

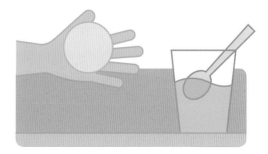

You will need...

- Baking sheet
- Butter
- Paper towel
- Packet of instant mashed potato
- Kitchen scales

- Bowl
- Grater
- Teaspoon
- Baking tray
- Glass
- Tablespoon

- Cheese
- Kettle
- Tomato ketchup
- Ruler
- Water
- Oven mitts

5 Grate enough cheese to cover two potato moons. Gently roll them in the cheese. You may need to re-shape them.

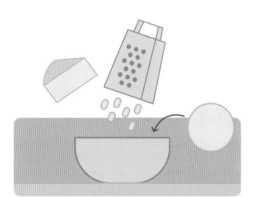

6 Use the back of the teaspoon to rub tomato ketchup over your other two potato moons.

⚠️ **MESS WARNING!** Don't forget to wash up afterward!

Using a tablespoon, place the potato moons on the baking tray. Ask an adult to put the tray in the oven at 375°F (190°C) for 40 minutes, then take them out.

ASK AN ADULT

What do you notice about your alien moons? Have they changed size, and are they still round, or have alien forces been at work? Enjoy eating them!

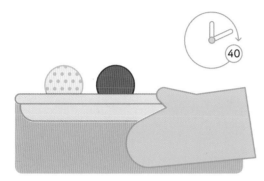

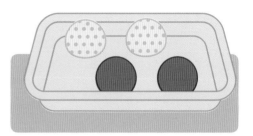

DID YOU KNOW?

The temperature at which cheese melts depends on how much water it contains. Very soft, watery cheeses, such as mozzarella, melt at a lower temperature than harder, drier cheeses such as Cheddar.

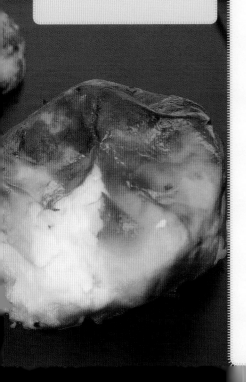

The Science:
COOKING CHEMISTRY, MOONS, AND CHEESE

In the oven, the browning chemical reaction (see page 51) turns the potato and cheese a golden brown color. But first the cheese melts. Cheese is curdled milk and it contains milk fat and protein. As the cheese gets hotter, the fat droplets and the bonds holding protein molecules together break apart. The cheese turns into a gooey liquid. As the cheese cools, it becomes solid again.

Moons are natural objects that orbit (go around) planets. Earth's Moon isn't made of cheese, but there's one moon in our Solar System that really does look cheesy! It's called Io, and it orbits the planet Jupiter. Just as your edible alien moons are covered in hot, melted cheese, so parts of Io are covered in hot, molten rock, or lava, which comes from giant volcanoes.

Earth's Moon has no active volcanoes and most of the time it looks like your uncooked potato moons. But sometimes it turns red like a ketchup moon! This happens when Earth passes between the Sun and the Moon, and you see Earth's shadow on the Moon's surface. The red color is sunlight that passed through Earth's atmosphere (see page 15). We see it as red because the Moon reflects the red light back to Earth.

Io

Earth's Moon

PERFECT PIZZA SCIENCE

Most people love pizza, but not many people know its science secrets. Follow this recipe to discover the science, and end up with a perfect pizza!

MESS WARNING!
Don't forget to clean and tidy your mess as you go, and wash up afterward!

WARNING!
The pizza will be HOT when it comes out of the oven—wait for it to cool before you eat it.

1 Fill a glass with 7 ounces (200 ml) of warm water (no hotter than bath water.)

2 Add one teaspoon of sugar to the warm water and stir until it dissolves. Pour in a packet of dried yeast and stir well.

3 Wait 15–20 minutes, stirring occasionally if the mixture appears to separate. The mixture will get frothy.

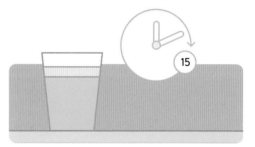

4 Ask an adult to slice the mozzarella cheese fairly thinly, and to chop the tomatoes and any other toppings you would like on your pizza.

You could use a can of chopped tomatoes instead of fresh tomatoes and tomato purée.

You will need...

- Mixing bowl
- Glass
- Knife
- 2 baking trays
- Clean tea towel
- Wooden spoon for mixing
- Rolling pin

- Water
- Measuring cup
- Kitchen scales
- Ruler
- Strong white flour or special pizza flour
- Packet of dried yeast
- Salt

- Other toppings, such as herbs and mushrooms
- Concentrated tomato purée
- Olive oil
- Sugar
- Tomatoes

- Mozzarella cheese
- Teaspoon
- Tablespoon
- Chopping board
- Paper towel

5 While your adult helper is chopping, add 2 ½ cups (300 g) of strong white flour or special pizza flour to a mixing bowl and stir in one tablespoon of olive oil and a pinch of salt.

6 When the yeast mixture is ready, make a hole in the middle of the flour and pour in the mixture. Stir until the water and flour form a thick, sticky, well-mixed ball of dough.

7 Sprinkle a little flour on your hands and on the clean work surface. Flatten the dough and push it into a ball repeatedly for five minutes. This is called kneading the dough.

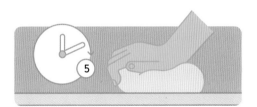

8 Sprinkle a little flour onto the work surface. Divide the dough into two balls. Use the rolling pin to roll each ball into a thin pizza about 12 inches (30 cm) across.

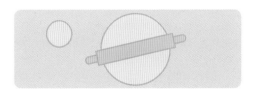

9 Using a paper towel, smear a little olive oil over two baking sheets. Lay a pizza on each sheet and ask your adult helper to heat the oven to 450ºF (230ºC).

ASK AN ADULT

10 Use the back of a tablespoon to spread tomato purée over each pizza base. Then add chopped tomatoes, slices of mozzarella, and your chosen toppings. Drizzle a little olive oil over the pizzas.

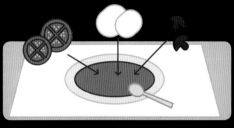

11 Ask an adult to put the pizzas in the oven. They should take them out after 10 minutes, or when the pizza bases are crisp and turning brown. In what ways has the pizza dough changed since step 6?

ASK AN ADULT

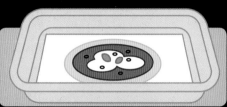

CONGRATULATIONS!
You've made TWO pizzas. There should be plenty to share with your friends or family!

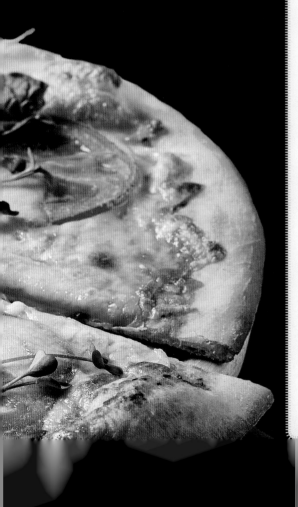

The Science:
YEAST, DOUGH, AND MELTED CHEESE

This experiment may sound like cooking —and it is!—but it's stuffed with lots of science, too.

Take yeast, for example. This curious powder is actually thousands of microscopic lifeforms. Each one is a living **cell**. Like most living things, yeast cells need water, food, and warmth, and that's what you give them in this experiment. As they feed on the sugar, they produce carbon dioxide gas that bubbles up and makes the yeast mixture frothy.

Once in the dough, the yeast cells keep feeding and pumping out gas. This makes the dough swell, even in the oven. After a while the heat kills off the yeast cells, but don't feel too sorry for them. They've done a great job!

In the oven, the browning chemical reaction (see page 51) makes the pizza brown and crispy. Meanwhile, the cheese melts (see page 61). Your adult helper sliced the cheese thinly to ensure that the cheese would heat evenly and melt quickly. The heat passes from the outside to the inside of the cheese, so thinly sliced or grated cheese heats up faster. That's why you grated the cheese on page 59.

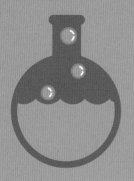

TASTE TEST

Have you ever wondered why good food and drink tastes s-o-o GOOD? Say "thanks" to your nose! Find out how taste and smell are related in this fun taste test experiment.

1 Put 2 ounces (60 ml) of lemon juice into a glass. Add ¾ cup (200 ml) of water and stir well.

2 Take a second glass and add 2 ounces (60 ml) of grape soda. In the third glass, pour in 2 ounces (60 ml) of orange soda. Add 5 ounces (150 ml) of water to both and stir well. Fill the fourth glass with fresh water.

3 **ASK AN ADULT** Cover your eyes and hold your nose. Ask an adult to pass you the three flavored drinks, one at a time, without telling you which is which. They may try to fool you by dropping false hints! Take a sip of each drink, followed by a mouthful of water. Can you identify all of them?

4 Repeat step 3, but this time sniff the drinks before you sip them. What do you notice?

DID YOU KNOW?

You sense taste using taste buds on your tongue, sides of mouth, and top of throat.

You will need...

- Four glasses
- Measuring cup
- Teaspoon
- Orange soda
- Grape soda
- Lemon juice
- Water

The Science:
TASTE AND SMELL

The aim of the experiment is to show how your senses of taste and smell work together when you eat and drink. Each taste bud in your mouth contains sensor cells that react to one of five tastes: sweet, sour, salty, bitter, and umami (meaty). At the same time, sensor cells in your nose detect flavor molecules rising up from your food and drink. This is your sense of smell, which is about TEN THOUSAND times more sensitive than your sense of taste!

Red grape juice and orange soda both taste sweet, but without your sense of smell it's quite hard to tell them apart. Lemon juice has a strong, sharp, sour taste that you can identify even without sniffing it.

ICE COLORS

Cold stuff is just as much fun as the hot stuff, and just as scientific, too! Let's get started by making curiously colorful ice...

> **MESS WARNING!**
> Food coloring stains—wear old clothes!
> Put down newspaper to catch any colored spills or drips.

> **WARNING!**
> DON'T drink the salty ice water.
> DON'T touch or hold the ice straight from the freezer—it could be as cold as −4°F (−20°C), and could cause cold "burns."

1 Fill a large plastic bottle with water and leave it overnight in the freezer.

2 Ask an adult helper to cut open the bottle using a knife or scissors. The adult should wear gloves to remove the ice and place it on a plastic tray.

ASK AN ADULT

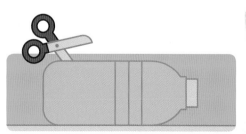

3 Half-fill a spray container with warm water. Pour some salt onto a small area of the ice block. Spray the salt with warm water. Watch what happens.

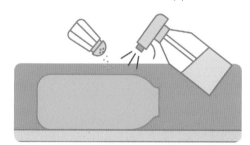

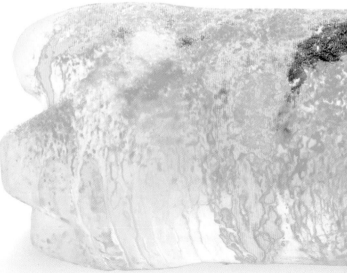

You will need...

- Water
- Measuring cup
- Squeeze spray container
- Knife or scissors
- Salt
- Plastic tray
- Food coloring (as many colors as you like)
- Magnifying glass
- Large plastic bottle
- Gloves

4 Repeat step 3 on different parts of the ice block.

5 The ice will start to melt where you sprayed it. Now drip different food colorings onto the ice to make some spectacular effects.

A crust of salt crystals may form on the ice. You can study these under a magnifying glass, then wipe them off with a cloth.

The Science: FREEZING POINT

Inside your lump of ice, water molecules join together to make a solid substance—frozen water. This happens at 32°F (0°C), the normal freezing point of water.

But ice is always trying to melt, so it has a thin layer of water around it. When you pour salt on the ice, the salt dissolves in the water. Spraying warm water on the ice helps to speed up the melting. The atoms in the salt stop the water molecules from freezing back into ice. To re-freeze, the salty ice would need to be colder than 32°F (0°C).

Because your ice can't refreeze, it melts faster than normal. Tiny pits form on the surface as it melts, and the food coloring runs into these, showing just how much the ice has melted.

FROSTY MOMENTS

Your kitchen lab isn't always hot and steamy. In this FROSTY experiment, find out how to turn water vapor into ice.

1 Ask an adult helper to remove the lid and any sharp edges from an aluminum can, and wash it until it's clean.

ASK AN ADULT

2 Take a resealable plastic bag and fill it with enough ice cubes to half fill the can. Ask your adult helper to seal the bag and hit the ice cubes with a rubber mallet, just hard enough to break them up without making any holes in the bag.

ASK AN ADULT

ASK AN ADULT

If the frost is slow to appear, you can speed things up by asking an adult to place a mug of nearly boiling water about 6 inches (15 cm) from the can.

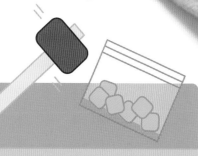

You will need...

- Aluminum can
- Ice cubes
- Gloves
- Medium resealable plastic bag
- Rubber mallet
- Paper towel
- Salt
- Magnifying glass
- Dessert spoon

3 Pour half the crushed ice cubes into the can. Add a dessert spoon of salt. Repeat. Moisten the paper towel and stand the can on it.

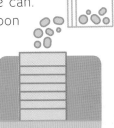

4 Look at the sides of the can under a magnifying glass after 20, 40, and 60 minutes. What do you see?

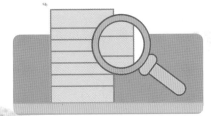

DID YOU KNOW?

On the dwarf planet Pluto, there are knife-like frost ridges as high as skyscrapers. But this isn't water frost—the ridges are made of frozen methane.

The Science:
CONDENSATION AND FROST

This experiment shows you how to turn water vapor (see page 55) into ice. There's always some water vapor in the air in your kitchen lab, and more floats up from the moist paper towel. As the water vapor comes near the cold can, the water molecules cool. They form liquid water droplets. This process is called **condensation**. When the droplets land on the can, they freeze to form frost. When you look at the frost through the magnifying glass, you can see that it's made up of tiny ice crystals.

But what makes the can's surface so cold? Ice is cold, of course, and by adding salt, you lower its freezing point and speed up melting (see page 69). As the ice melts, it draws heat from the water and the metal can. This makes the can cold enough to freeze water on the outside of the aluminum into frost. Metal is a good **conductor** of heat —its atoms are good at passing on heat.

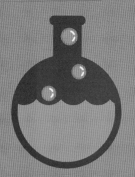

NICE CREAM

Question: What's nicer than a delicious dish of ice cream? Answer: a delicious dish of homemade scientific ice cream! Let's make some!

WARNING!
⚠ Handling ice can burn fingers. Ask your adult helper to wear gloves.

1 Pour ¹/₂ cup (120 ml) of heavy cream into a measuring cup. Add ¹/₂ cup (120 ml) of milk, one tablespoon of sugar, and half a teaspoon of vanilla essence. Pour the mixture into the smaller bag. Seal the bag and shake it.

2 Ask an adult to half-fill a medium resealable plastic bag with ice cubes and hit it with a rubber mallet to crush the ice.

ASK AN ADULT

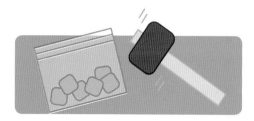

3 Add eight tablespoons of salt to the crushed ice. Place the smaller bag with the ice-cream mixture inside the medium bag and seal the medium bag. Place the medium bag inside a second medium resealable plastic bag and seal this too.

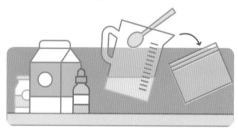

4 Wearing gloves, shake and squish the bags with your fingers for 12 minutes or until all the ice has melted in the medium bag. The longer you shake and squish, the creamier the mixture will become.

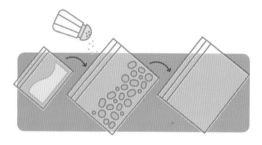

You will need...

- Gloves
- Tea towel
- Salt
- Heavy cream
- Whole milk
- Vanilla essence

- Dessert spoon
- Plastic container
- Ice cubes
- Caster sugar
- Tablespoon
- Teaspoon

- Plastic bowl
- Measuring cup
- 2 medium resealable plastic bags
- 1 small resealable plastic bag
- Rubber mallet

5 Open the two medium bags and lift out the smaller bag. Rinse the salt off it and turn out the ice cream into a plastic container. Pop some in a bowl to eat, or use it to make the recipe on pages 74–77.

The Science:
ICE CREAM: FREEZING AND MIXING

We know salt makes ice melt faster (page 69). Melting requires heat, so as the ice melts, it draws heat from the small bag. This makes the ice-cream mixture freeze.

You shake and squish the mixture to mix the ingredients. Squishing ensures that the ice crystals in the ice cream are small, so the mixture is smoother and less grainy. Shaking mixes the sugar with the fat (in the cream and milk) and the protein (in the milk), giving a creamy texture. The sugar adds sweetness and, like salt, ensures that the ice cream melts more quickly. This means it isn't too cold when you eat it. If it was too cold, you wouldn't be able to taste it and it might hurt your mouth. Vanilla gives the ice cream its flavor. Shaking and squishing also mixes in air, which keeps your ice cream light.

BAKED
ICE CREAM

Surely hot ice cream is against the laws of science?
WRONG! Here's how to bake the impossible. You
can have fun with the shape, too – see page 76!

1 Line a baking tray with
aluminum foil.

2 Wash and dry your hands.

3 Place a cookie on the foil-covered
tray. Alternatively you could use a
flan case cut to about the same
size as a cookie.

If your eggs have been
stored in the fridge, take
them out and leave them
to warm up at room
temperature for about
two hours before you
use them.

4 Take three fresh, room-temperature
eggs. To separate the yolks and
whites, crack an egg on the rim of
a bowl and break it open over the
jug. Spoon out the yolk without
breaking it, and put it in a glass.
Pour the egg white into the bowl.

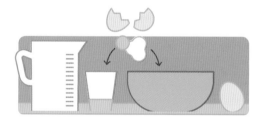

5 Repeat for each egg. Make sure
NO egg yolk mixes with the whites.

6 Ask an adult to beat the
mixture with an electric whisk
for exactly 50 seconds. The
egg whites will be very foamy.

ASK AN
ADULT

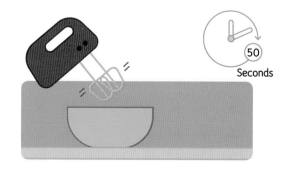

50
Seconds

- Baking tray
- Aluminum foil
- Large, thick cookie
- Ice cream
  (not soft-scoop)
- 3 large eggs
  (ideally fresh eggs)
- Caster sugar
- Metal or glass bowl
- Jug
- Glass
- Electric whisk
- Kitchen scales
- Tablespoon
- Ice-cream scoop

7 Measure $^2/_3$ cup (150 g) of caster sugar and add it to the egg whites, one tablespoon at a time. Ask your adult helper to keep whisking at a slow speed until the mixture is glossy and forms very stiff peaks—this may take 10 minutes.

ASK AN ADULT

8 Place a dome-shaped scoop of ice cream on top of the cookie.

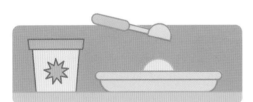

An ice-cream scoop is ideal for step 8. Do not use soft-scoop ice cream. Instead of store-bought ice cream you could use your homemade ice cream from pages 72–73!

9 Cover the ice cream and cookie completely in egg white mixture. Take care not to leave any gaps.

10 Place the dessert in the freezer for at least one hour.

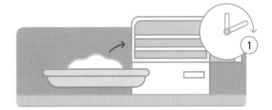

11 Ask an adult to set the oven to 450°F (230°C) and put the dessert in the hot oven. He or she should take it out after about five minutes, once the mixture has browned slightly.

ASK AN ADULT

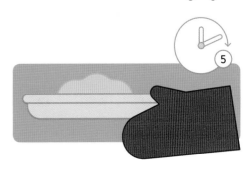

You could use cake stickers for your creature's feet and eyes—you can buy cake stickers from kitchen stores—or you could make them from icing.

CHILLY CREATURE CHALLENGE

Can you make a cooked ice-cream creature like this one? You can make the spikes by dipping the back of your spoon into the meringue and lifting it up. (Don't forget to check at step 7 that the mixture is forming very stiff peaks.)

The Science:
PROTEIN AND INSULATORS

So why hasn't the ice cream melted in the hot oven? And what has happened to the egg white mixture? Let's start with the egg white, which is about 92 percent water and 8 percent protein. The proteins are made up of chains of amino acids (see page 51)—each protein is like a ball of string floating in water. The outer layers of string are amino acids attracted to water, and on the inside are amino acids that push away water. Whisking the egg white mixes in air. Since some amino acids push away water, air bubbles get trapped among the amino acids. The protein molecules start to unravel, but then knit together in a kind of mesh around the bubbles.

Next you added sugar. The sugar dissolves in the egg white foam and thickens the mixture, making it stretchy.

Heating makes a lot of water evaporate, but the protein mesh and stretchy mixture keeps the bubbles in place. In fact, heating makes the bubbles stronger by tightening the bonds linking the protein molecules. The heat is enough to trigger the browning chemical reaction (see page 51) on the outside of the meringue.

The meringue bubbles stop the ice cream from melting. They contain air, and air doesn't let heat pass through it easily—it is a good **insulator**. The air bubbles protect the ice cream from the heat of the oven.

The final word:
EDIBLE SCIENCE

If you've just tried the experiments in this book, you'll know that food and drink are packed with crucial chemistry and surprising science just begging to be discovered. Why not cook up your very own edible experiments? It's your chance to enjoy science—and eat it too!

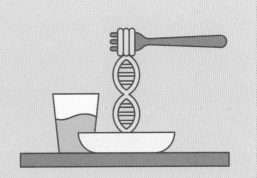

GLOSSARY

Acid – a type of chemical. When mixed with water, strong acids can dissolve other substances.

Alkali – a special kind of base that dissolves in water to make an alkaline solution. Like strong acids, strong alkaline solutions are able to dissolve other substances.

Atmosphere – the mixture of gases around a planet such as Earth.

Base – a type of chemical that can neutralize acids.

Carbon dioxide – a gas with molecules made up of a carbon atom and two oxygen atoms bonded together. Your body makes carbon dioxide in every living cell as it releases energy from food during respiration. We get rid of carbon dioxide in the air we breathe out.

Cell – a living unit. All animals and plants are made of cells.

Charged – Having a positive or negative electric charge. Charged particles with the same charge repel each other; those with unlike charges attract. An electric current is a flow of electric charge.

Chemical reaction – the process when two or more chemicals combine to make a new molecule or molecules. Some chemical reactions can be reversed, but others can't.

Conductor – a material that allows heat or electricity to pass through it.

Crystal – a substance where the atoms or molecules are arranged in a regular pattern. Crystals in your kitchen lab include salt, sugar, and ice.

Condensation – when vapor cools to form liquid droplets. Condensation is the opposite of evaporation. Clouds are made of water droplets formed by condensation.

Dense/density – the amount of matter compared with the space it takes up. You can calculate the density of an object or a material by dividing its mass by its volume.

Evaporation – when a liquid warms and turns to vapor. Puddles dry up because of evaporation.

Friction – the force created when two objects rub against each other. Friction often slows down moving objects and turns their energy into heat.

Inertia – the quality that keeps an object either still or moving in a straight line. The more matter an object contains, the more inertia it has.

Insulator – a material that heat or electricity cannot pass through easily.

Mass – the amount of matter (material) that an object contains.

Molecule – group of atoms bonded together. Most chemicals are made of molecules.

Neutral – a chemical that isn't an acid or a base—it's in-between. Pure water is a neutral chemical.

Protein – a type of molecule made of chains of smaller molecules called amino acids. You need to eat protein in order to grow and stay healthy. Proteins are found in many foods and all animals and plants.

Viscosity – how much a fluid resists attempts to stir it or make it change shape. Viscous liquids are thick and some appear almost solid.

INDEX

acids 41, 45, 49
air pressure 26-27, 53
alkalis 41, 49
atmosphere 15

baked ice cream 74-77
baking soda 40-41,
  56-57
bases 41
bread 50-51
browning 50-51, 59-61
bubbles 25, 45, 46-47, 53, 57
buoyancy 24-25
butter 8-9

candies, giant 16-17, 52-53
caramelization 53, 54-55
cells 65
cellulose 12-13
cheese 58-61, 62-65
color change 40-41
condensation 70-71
cornstarch 10-11
cream 8-9, 72-73
crystals 55
curds 61

density 20-21, 22-23
detergent 32-33, 39, 47, 49
diffusion 16-17
dough 62-65

eggs
  giant 42-45
  meringue 74-77
evaporation 55

fat 8-9, 39
floating 20-21, 22-23, 24-25,
  32-33

flour 12-13
fluids 10-11
foam 46-47
freezing 68-69, 70-71, 72-73
friction 37

gelatine 16-17, 53
glowing 45
glue 12-13
gravy 55

hydrometer 22-23

ice 68-69, 70-71
ice cream 72-73, 74-77
indicators 41
inertia 37
insulation 77

lemonade 24-25
lemons 48-49
light 14-15, 51, 61
liquids
  color change 40-41
  density 20-21, 22-23
  freezing 68-69, 70-71
  non-Newtonian fluids 10-11
  surface tension 28-31, 33,
    38-39, 47
  whirlpools 34-35

marshmallows 52-53
meringue 74-77
milk 14-15, 38-39, 61
mixing 18-19, 38-39, 72-73
moons 61
mummies, Egyptian 56
mustard 18-19

Newton, Isaac 11, 37

non-Newtonian fluids 10-11
oil 18-19, 34-35
osmosis 45

pizza 62-65
potato moons 58-61
pressure 26-27, 53
protein 8-9, 51, 61, 77

raisins 24-25

safety 7
salad dressings 18-19
salt 68-69, 70-71, 72-73
sinking 22-23, 32-33
smell 66-67
solids 10-11
starch 12-13, 51
sugar 54-55, 56-57
sunsets 14-15
surface tension 30-31, 33, 39, 4

table trick 36-37
taste 66-67
toast 50-51

upthrust 21, 22-23, 25

vinegar 18-19, 42-45, 61
viscosity 11
volcanoes 48-49, 56-57
vortex 34-35

water 22-23, 28-31, 34-35,
  68-69
whirlpools 34-35

yeast 62-65